CONTENTS

Standing on the Threshold
of
Madness

by
Benjamin Blake

PARALLEL UNIVERSE PUBLICATIONS

Parallel Universe Publications
First Published in the UK in 2017
Copyright © 2017 Benjamin Blake
Cover design © 2017

Vulpes Vulpes, Near-Death Experiences, Cataclysmic Scan, and *Spectral Tides* were first published in *The Red Morgue Journal* (R.I.P.)

ISBN: 978-0-9957173-1-2
Parallel Universe Publications, 130 Union Road,
Oswaldtwistle, Lancashire, BB5 3DR, UK

For S.A. Wales

A Return

The sound travels furthest at night
Over empty fields
And lonely farm houses
The flap of leathery wings
Forewarns of my return

This coastal city
Knows my name
Though they dare only speak
In hushed whispers
Born at the unholy hour
One midwinter night
Many years ago

The old stone church
Now sits boarded up
The nave gathering dust
But there are always new maidens
I shall drink of their blood
The one from my homelands
Stripped bare beneath the cold stars
Waxen skin bathed in the moon's soft glow
She will be found come morning
Laid out like so many
Before her
Though, if fortuitous, she will wake
When the sun sinks in fallow ground
Blessed with this eternal curse

Descent of Avernus

These scrawled demons
Reach out with ink-stained hands
As I continue to fall deeper
Into darkened soil

Tree roots coil themselves
Around a clawed neck
Itching for a hanging forthwith
Only I know what these arcane symbols mean
And they shall never be translated

The clock ticks in sanguine time
Its face shattered
Its original intention obsolete
The telephone speaks in tongues
Between bursts of unbearable static

Watched over by old gods
As these charred bones walk through hellfire
Never losing count
Of the near-futile steps
It takes to cross
This infernal lake

Days stretch eternal
In this unholy place
Never wavering
Nor relinquishing
Their deathly hold

This nightmare knows no waking
Only the final verdict
In the spent shells
Of the Devil's firing squad

Coven

A flame is extinguished
In the still of night
Another is ignited
And with it comes clandestine sentences
Spoken in a foreign tongue

This cloaked closed circle
Watches with wary eyes from afar
Spells of protection
Incantations only uttered
Behind doors always closed

A bat is caught mid-flight
And kissed upon the mouth
Before being released
Into a blood red sky

Already they know this unhallowed name
Head bowed, I stand before the unseen jury
I offer up this woodcut flesh
For the final daughter
To sink claws and teeth into
And devour at her will

Sacrosanct

There was someone else in the photograph
I opened my eyes and mind to the Devil
Yesterday was two days ago
Now I wither in glorious solitude
Waiting for a fitful tomorrow

Books and knives
I cut the inscription from the binding
Tore at the mouth that breathed without bleeding
And set fire to the nightstand

Demonic possession
Is a national pastime
Like baseball, like wrist-cutting
Celluloid front window mannequins
Dance to next year's songs
And melt into perfect puddles

An esoteric drunk
An exorcist out of work
What will spill forth from this stained palette?
This planchette will spell it all out
Eventually

Where the Dead Come to Party

The record player keeps coming alive at night
Along with the living room lights
And the television set

Every once in a while
Something darkened rattles out of the faucet
And a foreign object is discovered somewhere
Where it definitely should not be found

Bedsheets stripped from the sleeping
A cold hand on a warm thigh
The sound of heavy breathing
Coming faintly from the bedroom closet

Somebody call a priest
And the furniture movers
This is too much for the living to bear

Bear Skin Rug

Perpetually snarling maw
She sits upon the fur
Nude, but for a simple necklace
Oh, what wonders wait behind that locked door!
Sepia-tone skin and misplaced eyes
The whir of a 35mm camera
Capturing these sanguine moments
For a small eternity
Those curves sever limbs
And deep inside
I am already dead

Shadow Fire

A house, engulfed in black flame
Ensconced in a new night
The stars fade out behind
Plumes of billowing smoke
Inverted shrieks tear from collapsing walls
Crescending into an earth-shaking cacophony

The circle binds
Leaving no escape
Soon there will be nothing left
But ash

Before Dawn

A horse thunders through the chill of the November night
Its rider hunched forward
The wind whips relentless
Cold rain slicing his face
The trees have become amorphous
And seconds feel like hours

Word came via telegram
Of her fearful sinking
Will he be greeted by a new cadaver?
Or is there still time?

Lightning renders the sky asunder
The rain falls harder
Legs and hooves thick with mud and mire
Spittle gathers at the mouth
He digs the spurs in
Clenches teeth
And narrows reddened eyes

The house reads deserted
The staircase seems to keep growing
Portraits laugh with sickening mirth
The cat is scornful
And crouches beneath a dresser

The bedroom door is ajar
She lies dead still
Doctor at side
And priest at foot
The last rites have just been read

Studies in Occultism

Black candles burn
Their loving light
Casting dancing shadows
Upon the bedroom wall

Words are spoken
In a hushed whisper
Symbols drawn
With an oak branch finger

Pennies are buried
With salt and satin
A photograph is set aflame
Handwritten inscription on the underside
Energy is expended
In a cataclysmic climax

And in a future hour
She falls stricken
With a mysterious malady

Vortex Club

Wrapped in red curtain
Only the polished toes of a pair of leather shoes
Protruding from the bottom
An urn stands on a plinth to the left
Ashes nestled safely inside
To the right, is a small glass ball
Clutched in a clawed foot
Her breathing comes whispered and tight
As she dances across the carpeted floor
Gyrating to the pulse of a song
Sung in the key of Despair
Where has your torso gone?
Below, below, below
Where were your fingers
When he took you in the brook?
The letter-opener was used ingeniously
While she covered her eyes with her hands
Now the toes tap to the rhythm

Porchlight

Sometimes the night stands dead still
Those rare silent moments
That are only broken by the hoot of an owl
Or the rustling of some other nocturnal creature

The kind of night where the smoke from your cigarette
Carries in the chill of the air
Drifting no which way in particular
Seclusion makes the utmost sense at times like these
And sleep will come easy
When it is time

Epitaphs as Epilogues

I grew up in a ghost town
My haunts its empty streets
And vacant storefronts
A woodland park for wandering children
Lost save for fragments of rudimentary maps
Scrawled on old pieces of scrap paper
A past path that led to riverside misadventures
The buzzing of bees in a hollowed trunk
Swarming in the still winter air
As she sunk into rotting leaves
Beneath the bent and gnarled
Branches of contorted willows
A bramble thorn pricked her finger
As she reached out
Blood was drawn
But not as it should have been
I was only an innocent then
As much as I ever was

A Cemetery Cat

All Hallows' Eve
Feline paw upon crumbling stone
Eyes moon-yellow
Fangs bared
with midnight hiss

An angel perpetually weeps
A chiselled name now forgotten
A brush of black tail along ivy
A dry rattle amongst deadened leaves
The solitary mourner
Crossing paths with wayward priests
& love-stricken youths

The mist rolls in
As she rises from her slumber
Sets out to stalk her unsuspecting prey
Over the crooked wall
And under weathered gate
She makes her way to an open window
A soft orange glow emanating from within
She pauses upon the sill
Before leaping and landing
On the flower-patterned carpet
Of the first floor nursery room

Broken Clock

A crash of lightning
Wrenched me from the arms of sleep
Reaching out to the nightstand
I knocked my clock onto the hardwood floor
Where its face broke
And it froze at 3 a.m.

The cry of far-off sirens
Rang out as I struggled to get dressed
Possessed with an inexplicable knowledge
That I had to get out of the house

The cold rain began to fall
As I hurried across the front lawn
Everyone else was still fast asleep

At the end of the street
I heard the shots ring out
The morning paper read:
FOUR DEAD IN FAMILY MASSACRE
It should have been five

Something Hidden

Fire dances in eyes of pearl
Hinting at secrets
Only told in the dead of night
Discarded hosiery reveals the palest of skin
Its smoothness enough
To make any man
Die a little inside

The animals watch from the shadows
With teeth bared and claws poised
A night bird takes flight from the ensconcing woodlands
Its shriek piercing through the firs
Her mouth opens
And delicate words seep out

Tiny razor-sharp teeth
Pierce a wrist
The blood flows warm and true
Rivulets run down her cheeks and chin
Her lithe neck
And between pert perfect breasts
I lie exsanguinated

Burning Churches, Burning Lives

That old familiar feeling
Like a shotgun blast to the abdomen
A gaze that impales
And hands that claw at a shuttered chest
Until the bone has worn thin

I have died a thousand little deaths
At the hands of strangers

Endless

At night the forest is filled with strange sounds
I walk alone
No stranger to its midnight murmurings
For centuries now
My kind has roamed these worn trails
Guided by the light of the moon
And the inherent pull of the hunt
A new prey
To pry open like a hitherto forgotten chest
They are not aware of our existence
And never will be
Faint impressions left by footfalls
Is all that tells of these otherworldly excursions
Alongside the bones that are picked clean
And scattered to the four winds

To Lay with Wolves

Yellow fang
Where do you keep your appetite?
So honest, so insatiable
I have grown considerably weakened
From pulling these arrowheads from my flesh
A circle of sticks
Form a frame around the unsuspecting quarry
O, to taste like I used to
To tear ligament and bone
Like you
Dine upon blood-painted snow
To later fall asleep
As the campfire dances
In our swiftly-closing eyes
Resting heavy heads
Upon wary paws
With full stomachs
And sated hearts

A Darker Heart

Light bleeds
Through the stained-glass windows
Of the ancient stone church
Slightly suffusing the worn stones
One of which you crouch behind
A shadow within a shadow
Nearing the end
Of many a season of searching

Silent as a creeping cat
You make your way down the nave
The priest stands stooped over the altar
Utterly oblivious
That he is the quarry

Sagging skin bulges over garrotte wire
As surprised eyes strain from sockets
Liver-spotted hands scrabble in futile self-preservation
As the life slowly drains from lecherous limbs
There is always room for one more
In the old bone orchard
Your work here is done

Candleflame

She sits dead still
In a windowless room
Somewhere in the dead of night

Incessantly fingering her dead grandmother's rosary
Mouth nothing but a slit in a stoic face
Inkwell eyes, hair damp and lifeless
A skeleton draped in skin

She was beautiful once
Though one would never believe it

The Witching Hour

Cobblestone streets
Weaving through dense fog
No sound save for the footfalls
That echo with each step

A doorway sits in shadow
Tendrils of mist
Twisting like searching fingertips
A brass knocker sits in wolf's maw
Waiting for that fateful touch

Sunken Eyes

The Atlantic crashes against the cliff face
She watches from an upstairs window
Intermittently illuminated by the lighthouse's beam
It has been many a lonesome year
Since she last caught sight of him
Time has its wicked way with us all

Lightning tears across the blackened night sky
She is about to retreat when something finally happens
The wind picks up, grows into a whirling crescendo
The lighthouse blinks out
She can make out a bluish glow amidst the heaving waves
A small boat is thrown about in the spray and foam
A man stumbling helplessly at its helm
She can hear his cries
As if he was in the very same room

Slowly sinking, 'til there's nothing visible
Aside from a lone arm
Breaking momentarily the tumultuous swell
She hurries down the stairs, and through the front door
Nightgown billowing, she makes her way
Across the storm-kissed grounds
To the edge of the cliff

She hurls her fragile body
Onto the seaweed-choked rocks below
The Atlantic claims her limp shell

Vulpes Vulpes

One paw in front of the other
Lone, after the shortest of summers
And now that the winter has set in proper
I am free yet again
To relish the morning chill
And sink these incisors into what flesh I wish

Through crooked copse
And over slate stone wall
The hounds will never catch me now
Church bells ring out over the nearby hamlet
But my kind won't find respite
In that hollow hallow place
Just keep creeping in the ever-deepening shadows
Until the onset of evening

No matter how far I stray
This crepuscular creature has a den
For which the heart calls home

Indian Burial Grounds

A black house stands
Over an endless hedge-maze
Take the wrong twists and turns
And you'll find yourself at the edge of a cliff
The ocean throwing itself upon the darkened rocks
below
And maybe you will too

There are places where time wears thin
In a circle of surrounding firs
Or at the feet of a crumbling statuette
Rosebushes that reach with thorny arms
Begging to embrace

Once the front doors gape wide
Then swallow you whole
You will find yourself
In corridors that don't seem to stay the same
Rooms that stink of past suicides
The elevator rattles straight down
To the burning coals of the boiler room

Visions of a shotgun wedding
Painting walls a new crimson
Severing conjugal ties
And ripe jugulars
Carpets can be replaced
The remnants of past lives
Will remain

A Little More Dead

That dago red
Feels good in these veins
Another sultry summer smile
Fading into fall's chilled touch
I'll keep draining these glasses
A divine exsanguination
Replenishing this exhumed corpse

Sinning softly, I'll skip these hearts like rope
Used to hang effigies from the rafters of that old haunted
house
Crafted from sycamore sticks and grapevine cut from
graveyard stones
And bearing a remarkable resemblance to...

A hound of hell off its leash
Sniffing around the high-heels of newfound starlets
Or aging actresses that never got the part
But never left the party

Like Fire

Tombstones for eyes
Stripped to the bone
She smiles
With teeth that clack like typewriter keys
I incinerate all around me

Barren

Waiting for the appearance of light
Vision doubled and blurred
Dense fog has rolled in
And smothered the outpatient
Like a new-born child

Smokestacks tower toward the heavens
Diffused and omniscient
The Morse-code stutterings
Of a once-latent God
Punctuate every dire corridor
The suicide of an entire nation
Still wouldn't be enough

The waiting room is on fire
And the nurses have all quit
Wheelchairs roll through rivers of blood
While a small boy sits in the corner
And gets lost in a book
Every once in a while
Something stops
And doesn't start
Back up again
Like life support
Like broken hearts

Mortifïen

A box of bones beneath the stairs
Covered with dust and quite forgotten
A stray limb washed up on a riverbank
A darker shade of purple
And nibbled at by several species of fish
A hospital room at midnight
A school for wayward girls that morning
A skull smashed in with a brick from a chimney that
fell some years before
A small child torn apart by hungry wolves
Stillborns
Still hearts
The rapist laughs before he is shot in the face
And the priest takes a handful of pills prescribed to
another man
A young lady is found with her throat cut
In a pool of congealing blood
She still looks relatively pretty
Death comes swift
And leaves even swifter

Shapeshifter

Woke up in a hotel room
In a strange small town
With no recollection of how I had actually gotten there
It is sometime in the morning
That much I can tell
Anything else is fair game
A matchbook falls to the floor
When I tug on my pants
A phone number is scrawled on the inside flap in a
stranger's hand
I call
No one answers

A slightly distorted reflection
Stares back from the grime of the bathroom mirror
There are what appear to be bite marks
On my neck and cheek

The sunlight hurts
As I stumble to where I see my car is parked
I find it unlocked
But why is the passenger seat coated in blood?
And to whom does that stray shoe belong?

I get in
Discover the keys are still in the ignition
Light a battered cigarette with a match
And get the hell out

Late Night Keepsakes

A basement room
Not unexpectedly low-lit
A small stool sits
Before a large table
Its surface littered
With newspaper clippings
And empty bourbon glasses
Each has its own unique story to tell
A further step in a transgressive transformation
These crooked teeth
Fit more snugly each day
The sinews beneath inked skin
Near-bursting with anticipation
The consummate dawn
Will come one month from now
With the rise of the full moon
The blood black beneath the midnight sun

O, Saint of Killers

With hands that ache
For the warmth of the spill
Tongue salivating
From the desire for hidden flesh
The blade tucked into this frayed overcoat
Is beginning to lose patience

Watching from a high stone window
Something stirs below
A lonely lowly chambermaid
Cloaked in soot and grime
Not an indelible tarnish
She will do for now

Blood runs down the cobblestones of the alley
Trickles along the cracks in rivulets
And pools in small dark puddles
In the shadows
I shudder with sweet relief

Dissolute

Lamplight bleeds throughout the room
The bedsheets are torn and stained
Hanging upside down
With a sickening smile
Plastered across this wanton face

The tell-tale scent
Of lust-smeared lace
Verse scrawled across the bathroom mirror
In a darker shade
Of red lipstick

Empty glasses rattling
To the national anthem of the dead
The Ouija board was left upon the living room floor
Along with her best evening dress
And my good intentions

Photographs of the Recently Departed

Funeral home smile
It's raining again
Upon these still streets
The cracked sidewalk

Crooked birds take flight
From dead-limb perches
High in the shadowed branches
Of grass-verge elms

Leaves crunch beneath
The director's two-tone shoes
As he strolls purposely up the front walk
No flowers grow outside
This time of year

The flashbulb bursts
In the cold tiled room
His subjects never smile

A Haunting of the Heart

Following a faint apparition
Up a set of twisting stairs
A soft flickering hand
Trails the wooden banister
Her dress flows behind
And I am a captive
To her unearthly beauty

She glides above the patterned carpet
Of the second floor hallway
Illuminating so gentle
The hanging portraits
I cannot tear my gaze from her
And wouldn't
Even if I could

Like always
She disappears into the master bedroom
And like always
Upon my hasty arrival
I find her gone

Her Bones Will be Found Years from Now

Rain falls upon
The empty morning grounds
Mist lingers at the fringes of perception
From a tower window
A pale face looms
Watches the lonely girl
Scurrying for shelter
A knowing smile appears

Faint breaths in the dead of night
He waits outside her chamber door
Crouched low like an animal
Knife in gloved hand

Blood splashes upon the four-poster bed
Soaking silk pillowslip and sheets
Her muffled screams
Don't even wake the dogs

Skeletal Cat

Teeth yellowed and sockets empty
Rattling bones about the town
A grotesque display of otherworldly knowledge
Still wearing the collar
And slaughtering small animals

A feline of churchyard lore
A name called by brave (or stupid) children
Bringing spoilt milk and spooked horses
Rooftop accidents and sudden turns
For the worse

A photograph exists
Hung behind the bar at the Dog & Duck
Subject obscured and pane cracked
But its validity affirmed
By many a village drunk

The old woman folk say it comes by quite often
The local vicar still casts backwards glances
Whilst walking home at night
A childhood habit
That never quite died

Some claim our cat curls in a tomb
Rising when the sunk does sink to feed
Upon the blood of sleeping infants
They may, or may not, be right

Aconitum

Desolate corridors of the heart
Run awash with poison blood
Wolf's bane can be difficult to detect
Turning away comes with good reason
Wounds can be licked
But some things are final

Normal Hill Cemetery

Cemetery stones
Sitting beneath layers of ice and snow
Strolling quietly alone, camera in hand
Trying to capture something unspoken

Life can be rediscovered
In the limbs of dead trees
And loved ones long gone

You have more in common with
These supine citizens
Than those who still walk around on two legs

Never let the wayfaring spirit stop wandering
Nothing much matters
In this cold, cruel world
So keep what is kindred
Locked deep inside
That flatlining heart

Accidental Lighthouses

Our tangled bodies
Crashing on rocks
Wet and limp

I lost you some time ago
But found you in flames
On the edge of that small Midwestern town
I drove you back to the West Coast

Our hands were tied
Bound with coarse rope
Scraps of torn letters
Folded and placed under swollen tongues

You have always been the fire
That keeps these bones warm in eternal winter
Death is welcome now

Carving Pumpkins

These October nights feel like home
Sugar and knives
VHS tape and dead nurses
An excitement welling
In the pit of one's stomach
Like stolen fireworks

The small town streets
Burn with candle-flame
Shadows flit in peripheral vision
Ochre leaves fall over the heads of little ghosts
And the fevered children of Satan

A man can come back from the dead
On a night like this

Ambulance Bay

Armed with a camera and a flashlight
We climbed the concrete steps
To the old hospital grounds
With breath held tight in two pairs of lungs
We swept the incandescent beam across the gravel lot
And dirty window panes

Detritus scattered & nooks piled high with dead leaves
Didn't quite deter us
Though the scuffling of a harried hedgehog
Caught us well off-guard
And speaking of such
They didn't seem to be making their rounds
Years before, a former inmate
Had damn near maimed us both
Though, we weren't acquainted then
And wouldn't be for another several seasons

The camera flash illuminates like manmade lightening
The historic buildings and unkempt shrubbery
Accompanied by the implicit feeling of being watched
It's not until arriving home
When your wife is inspecting the subsequent shots
That the discovery is made
Of a gnarled visage
Peering from a window of the nurses' quarters
Could this be the fabled Lady in Grey?
A late suicide, once found hanging from the shower rod
Or something older
And much more dark?

Speak Softly to the Dead

The lake lies silent and still
Its tranquil surface
Misleading in its beauty
For much darker secrets sit
On the mud of its bed

The roots of weeping willows
Reach down to hidden bone
Discarded blades rust
Alongside long lost hooks
Dead leaves drift in the shafts of light
Piercing the murky depths
Eventually settle again
In the hands of misplaced maidens

Speak softly to the dead
For they will rarely reply
But always listen

1692

Midnight familiars
Press paws to my side
Marked skin that assimilated the woodland spirit
Tasted foxglove upon forked tongue
Drawing symbols in dirt with a sycamore stick
To attract fecund handmaidens
Resting from the journey home
From the languid river

To be drowned in a lake of flame
Or submerged in stagnant ponds
Until this skin is charred
Or these bellowed lungs full
Is pennies enough
for the Ferryman

Transplanted Rituals

The beating of kettledrums
Stretched with human hide
The campfire flickers
Dances hypnotically to the primitive rhythm

An archaic chant is grunted
Passed down from generations past
A powder is thrown over the leaping flame
Its origin only known to the village elders

Eyes roll back in sockets
Ivory windows in midnight skin
The women shriek in discord
Flecks of red in their hissing spit

A fowl is brought forth
By a small boy child
In the other hand
He clutches a large machete
Its blade glinting in the firelight

He holds the squirming cock aloft
Its talons curled tight into his left palm
The chanting intensifies
Shrieking grows more piercing
Drums are beat with fury
With one fluid motion
He severs the head from the still flapping torso
Blood spurts into the miniature inferno
Those not drumming begin to dance
Stomping earth with naked feet

Kicking up dust with pink heels
Bones rattle, smoke swirls
And then, without any sign or warning

Everything stops
The fire dies down
And somewhere, not-too-far-away
A man awakes amidst silken sheets
Finds he cannot draw breath
Claws at the pain exploding
Inside his well-fleshed chest
Gasps and rattles
with newfound death

Solitary Drive

The sound of blacktop beneath the tires
And fall rain against the windshield
Womb-like interior, dark and threaded with laces of
smoke
It's 3 a.m., and the passing town is fast asleep
Apart from the glow of the headlights
The streetlamps are the only illumination

Leaving secrets buried far behind
I'll find a town in which no one knows my name
They won't find me there
I'll paint a smile upon my pallid face
And wear it with a wary pride
She'll fall far and hard
Whoever she will be
Then it will be time
To be on the road again

Broken Camera Lens

The wind whistles over washed-out fields
I have spent countless days searching
Amidst tall dead grass
And dust-smothered railway shacks
For any trace of her
Alive, or otherwise

A raven watches
Perched atop a weathered fencepost
His gaze is cold and direct
Suddenly distracted by something on the stones of the tracks
Flashing in the noontide sun

The carrion eater takes flight
As I approach
A fragment of glass
Convex and iridescent
Inherently, I know it belonged to her

This whole thing reeks of misplaced time
I am still no closer
This has gone on for years now
I don't believe it will ever end

Shortwave Transmissions from Tomorrow

The signal comes
Weak at first
But rapidly growing in strength
From this attic room
Of an old house
In the Pacific Northwest

A garbled voice of sorts
Intermittently punctuated
By presidential speeches
Snippets of science fiction shows
From the early '50s
And other assorted half-lost broadcasts

A futile attempt at a response
Little lights blink on and off on the dial
And out the small, round window
The stars seem to glimmer in time

Suddenly everything dies
The desk lamp, the radio, the quiet hum of the ceiling fan
On the wooded hillside
The brightest glow is growing
Pervading the surrounding pines
And trailing toward the skies

He rushes down the pulldown stairs
Through the quiet house
And out into the night

Returning three days later
With a misplaced sense of time
And strange markings
Upon the upper inner thigh

Retractable Claws

Nights comes swift
As the old familiar feeling
Churns in the pit of my stomach
Waxes and wanes
Shivers and shakes
Before building to a crescendo
of flesh-sick anticipation

I will take you were you lay
dead spiders and all

Lycanthrope

The moon rises above a small village
Its light shining through spider-leg tree tops
And reflecting in small darkened cottage windows

A cabin sits on the outskirts
Crafted from pine logs
And a self-imposed half-solitude, of sorts
Between its narrow walls a man transforms

Lumbering down a twisting trail
The scent of blood pervading the olfactory sense
Higher brain is long gone now
One that in the day he so dearly loved
Is now the bloodlust-soaked quarry

The front door splinters inward
She sits bolt-upright in bed
Reaches for her father's revolver
From where it rests upon the nightstand

The creature slows, head lowered
And begins to creep toward the bedroom door
As it sinks to tensed haunches, and springs to strike
Fangs bared, and eyes wild
She fires thrice at the hellhound's chest
It howls in pain and rage
Crashes through the bedroom window on exit
And lopes off into the chill of the November night

The next morning, her lover appears at her door
A bouquet of roses in hand

She wraps him in a desperate embrace
Over her pretty shoulder, he winces in slight discomfort
Before planting a soft kiss upon her neck

Southbound

I've developed quite the taste for blood
And it's not going away
Anytime soon

Those cornflower-blue eyes will be mine
Along with the fingers
On your left hand

A growing collection
Of past lives and knives
Another photograph
To tack upon the wall above the altar
To bask in the black candlelight
And the sickening love
Swelling inside of me
Like some demented child

Extinguished

A man on fire
Bones charred
Beneath blistering skin
Flames pouring from a mouth agape
Trails of smoke rising
From where the eyes once were

Life fuels the inferno
In all its hellish aspects
There is only one way out
And it leaves nothing but ash
To be scattered over a barren land
On the biting December wind

Reredos

The church is all but deserted
Waiting behind the altar
A bottle of Sacramental wine in one hand
And a blade in the other

Gentle footsteps softly echo down the nave
A man starts of genuflect in a velvet voice
An abhorrence so deep, so pure
Begins to rise in the pit of a sickened stomach

Stepping out and standing upon the chancel's edge
Scathed and unsheathed
He doesn't even look up
Until his head is wrenched back
And his throat slit from ear to ear
In one fluid motion

The blood pools upon the cold stone floor
As he swiftly bleeds out
Mouth still moving in futile prayer
He slumps to the ground
And I stroll to the narthex
A self-satisfied smile
Upon my iconoclastic countenance

Funereal Party

The typewriter keys
Clack out a rhythm
As skeletal jazzmen
Tap-dance across the wooden floorboards
A taxidermy owl perched upon a mounted branch
Nods its feathered head to and fro
In taciturn appreciation
We're putting the word out
Via pipe-smoke signals
Pop's popping cherry-flavoured tobacco in the bowl
While Ma's taking her rolling pin
To another wayward skull
Heads are spinning
From the bottle of moonshine
Those damn Norse gods
Are at it again
An all-access invitation to insanity
And we're not stopping
Till the sun comes up
And we're reduced to attic dust

Marble Eyes

Cemetery smile
Morning sun cast upon mourning grounds
The dead shift silently in their sleep
Undisturbed by the living
And the prying hands of God

Blood-warm flesh
A cut palm bleeds into a palm cut
By a pocket knife
So safe in archaic dreams
That I vowed I'd only ever awake
To another

From where we lay
The church hangs inverted
My skin still bears the pitchfork scars
And silver bullet wounds
From a decade before

Bare thighs sickly sweet
Tendrils of smoke
Curl toward the heavens
As I lift the fabric of her dress

Please disappear with me
The world that waits
Outside these high stone walls
Isn't worth waiting for
Just ask the field mouse
And sewer rat

Atonal

A crumbling church
Sits in deep woodlands
Its windows gone
Its steeple sagging
Vines creep over weathered weatherboard
And its front doors
Lay off their hinges
Its small boneyard is taken back by nature
Names and dates long forgotten
Markers worn, choked with lichen
A gnarled tree sits in one corner
It seems to characteristically weep
A small child wanders here one day
Lost
Slips through the rust-rough wrought iron gates
He is never seen again
Not alive, anyway

Dreams of Dead Children

Swallowed whole
Wallowing in self-deprecating gloom
Wrists clearly cut
It's much easier to bleed
Than to truly try

Dresses only lifted
For the creeping fingers of God
Detuned and distracted
On her knees for one last prayer
Before a belated bedtime

Helping the poor
As a poor excuse for honour
Hymns and unbroken hymens
Or, so she so adamantly says
A cacophony of deceit
Stagnates in the billowing lungs
Of the church choir

I am content in flames
But how about you?

Literati (cisa)

A small figure in an ink-scratched picture
Found fallen behind an antique armoire
Its Oriental origins are obscure
But any further elaboration cannot be made

Hung it on the master bedroom wall
Framed in maple that had been gathering ancient attic
dust
Step back, admiring newfound handiwork
The wife will be happy when she arrives home from
London
This is sure to put a smile upon her face

Not impressed by the art, or the attempts at
lovemaking
Drifting into the void of an exhausted sleep
She's still somewhere downstairs
Dreams of cherry blossoms and lotus flowers
A geisha with bleeding, hollowed-out eyes
She smiles, and hands you the deer horn knives

Post-Mortem

A final farewell
Carving a love heart in each wrist
Laying beneath her favourite tree
A letter left
In her dead left hand
It shall be sealed and stitched
Inside her empty chest
I will never forget her eyes

Renaming the Old Town

I took the cemetery road
A winding country lane
Past empty fields
And still farmhouses
That eventually led to the old boneyard

They tore down the Suicide House
With promises of starting anew
That I don't think will ever be fulfilled

A pilgrimage to the public library
To bestow a book upon the town
One written in family blood
That makes reference to the serpentine river
That runs through the haunted woodlands
If only by a childhood spectre

A rendezvous in the Rhododendron dell
With a brunette dressed all in black
And her formidable hound
Near a decade before
We would meet in similar fashion
To fill our lungs with smoke
And carnal desire
That lantern etched upon your skin
Helps light my way

A hospital disguised as a home
I found a photograph of my nurse upon the wall
And my best-friend's grandfather
Down the hall from mine

Hunched over an uneaten meal, bearded and frail
A classical piece playing on a small plastic radio
Your photograph framed upon the wall
He didn't recognize who I was

Sometimes, I don't either

Shutter-Click, Moments Before Shots Ring Out

City Park, 9:32 a.m.
Dead leaves death-rattle across frosted ground
A man stands, hands stuffed deep into trench-coat pockets
A small shaving-cut, dappled with dried blood
Is visible upon his right cheek

A new figure appears at the base of the monolith
Hat pulled low, over cold blue eyes
A cigarette is lit
With a brass-plated lighter

The men coalesce
Hands are shaken
Small type-written notes are passed from palm to palm
Questions are asked
But not quite answered
The microcassette in the Dictaphone is rolling

Somewhere nearby
The shutter-click of a camera can barely be heard
Above the congregating pigeons
And then a shot rings out
In the chill of the winter air

Unseen

Sink into this autumn-damp hollow
The mist will ensconce all
Upon the moors
These time-old killing fields
I shall take your maidenhead

Chestnut hair collecting leaves
As teeth sink into collar bone
Thighs pressed tight
Arms cut and pinned like Christ
Her face is nowhere to be seen

Blood seeps into cold soil
Half-moons of pale flesh through torn hosiery
There is no cure for this curse
But for poisoned tips
Or a warm gun

Winter

It's snowing in this heart
As I walk these empty streets
No letters, no new names
Just an absence of light
In any form

The hulking shadow
Of an abandoned factory
Draws me to its rusted metal doors
I step inside
A vast interior
The drip and echo
Stones scattered
Across the oil-stained floor
An engine hoist holds a seized relic
In its chains
And I stand beneath
Willing it to drop

Dilapidated Welcome Sign

The whole town has gone to hell
Houses continue to sag a little further each day
Store fronts are boarded up, plate-glass painted over
And all the pretty young girls
Have blossomed and swiftly rotted

Lawns have outgrown their keepers
Smashed letterboxes lay in splintered pieces
Upon the cracked sidewalk
Even the dogs have given up
Marking their respective territory

The park has transformed into wilderness
The playground now a trellis for creeper
The old lurker has pawned his trench coat
And started making arrangements for his funeral

What was once a thriving community
Is now just wasted ink on a forgotten roadmap
Tucked inside the driver's side door
Of a car that broke down years ago

An Ending

The locket rattled down the kitchen sink
It wasn't an accident

Photographs were snatched
From the shattered plates of broken frames
And abruptly set aflame

Best dresses
Flung from the third floor bedroom window
Catching on the rose thorns below

Torn pantyhose
A bloodied nose
Eyes turned black and blue
Deliberating on the razorblade
If only an earthquake
Would send this whole city
Straight into the ocean

Sociopathic Blues

I killed again
Thought heading out on the road would help
But it only made it worse
Sipping bitter black coffee in a truck stop
These same slightly shaking hands
Were wrapped around a pretty hitchhiker's throat
Not a half hour before

At this point
I don't even care
If I get caught

Damn neon sign keeps buzzing
And its light pierces the too-thin curtains
It's been a week now
And the urge is rising
Today I sharpened my knives
And realized I don't even know what town I'm in

The car slows to a stop
And she climbs in

Exoskeleton

The room fills with bugs
As I struggle to write by lamplight
Summer's heat can drive one to kill
Or at least mortally wound
I think it's time that I keep to myself
For an indefinite period of time
I'll hold my aging breath
Until the oak leaves start to turn
And the autumnal rain
Comes down in slicing sheets
By then, these hell-sent insects
Will have died a thousand deaths
While I'll be in the midst of preparation
For the forthcoming resurrection

The Scratching Hag

The fathomless depths
Of this foreshadowed lake
She reaches out from its murky bed
The island sunk years ago
Reclaimed by the place of restless spirits
The pine-log cabin along with it
The typewriter clicks out Morse code tappings long into the
night
As the moonlight filters through the undulating waves
The surrounding firs are wrenched in the sudden wind
The very air howling
Like a wounded wolf

Will I ever
Write my way
Out of this dark place?

Digitalis

Ingesting the plant of the fox
Found at the copse's edge
Heart-beat slowing
To a faint flutter against the chest
Her lips part
And she slowly sinks
Into the soft silk
Of her parents' bed

She will be found
With the coming evening
Blonde hair fanned
Over carefully arranged pillows
Her wedding dress will be her burial gown

Nameless

The buttons cut from a blouse with a switchblade knife
Undergarments torn asunder under the unforgiving light of
a hanging bare bulb
In some roach-kissed flophouse somewhere in Los Angeles

Always Leave One Alive

Second-floor lounge room
A hail of bullets
Blood painting the papered walls
A darker red

The hiss of breath
From a punctured lung
As a lone survivor
Crawls across the carpeted floor
His watery eyes pleading
Though, there really is no need

I hold a match to the tip of a Toscanelli
Shake it out
Let it fall
And turn and leave

Staccato

Staircases spiral from this turpentine heart
As I sigh with sweet release
Sunlight pours through dust-choked windows
And warms dead skin
As I lay dozing on lacklustre wooden floorboards
A cat-like yawn and stretch
Bones cracking in a crooked spine
And a smile skittering
Around the corners of a barbed-wire mouth
There are secrets written in the floral-patterned filigree
Of the water-damaged wallpaper
If you know where to look

Renounced

Cast out
Exhaling plumes of smoke
Another passage played backward
Crucifix inverted
And repentant
For the sins left uncommitted

There's no changing
This claw-scarred skin
I should have set fire
To those lily-white robes
And drowned you in the baptismal font
When I had half the chance

Wrapped in Celluloid Reel

Sepia-tone lake house
Cigarette-burnt
A young wife walking briskly backward
Up the front walk
Clasp-purse hugged tight to a pert chest
Copper hair in pretty waves

The shattered upstairs bedroom window rights itself
And the moon crawls back to where it came from
A Buick sedan reverses down the otherwise empty street
One can't make out who's behind the wheel

A Wasteland

Desolation never comes easy
Seasons seem to die as soon as they begin
Barely there
Though, that's nothing new
The hatchet I keep by the bedside
Has dulled with use
And I've misplaced the stone somewhere
Alongside my heart

An unexpected snowfall
Does little to appease
And the old ghosts
Have lost their charm

Maybe it's time
To let go of time
And step out into the wilderness
To let the elements do as they will

Cataclysmic Scan

Prosthetic limbs
Scattered across the dust-coated floor
Of an emergency room
Somewhere in Texas

The sun rises
Spilling daylight through the dust-smeared windows
"Are we the only ones left?"
The handgun's cold against her scarred thigh
"There's no way of knowing right now"
Our volition derailed some time ago

Pink flamingos and picket fences
Are nothing but car wrecks now
Headlines like:
MIAMI TAKEN OVER BY HAITIAN CULTURE
Take on a whole new meaning
The suits never could've predicted this one

They're coming across the desert now
With no need for water, or multivitamins
Even if the doors are sufficiently barricaded
They'll be crashing through the plate glass panes
I think we need to ask ourselves:
"Do we really want to live in a world like this?"
I'm not sure I'd have the answer

What Happened in Portland?

The phone was dead
Disconnected, like what you'd become
I couldn't shake the portentous feeling
That cut my insides to ribbons
Like a prized knife

The snow fell swift and drifted deep
As the spirits whispered your name
With frosted breath, they sang:
"Something happened"

I tumbled into the void of sudden loss
Crawling on bloodied palms
And shattered knees
Across the stained carpet
To the gaping clothes closet
The rail bent beneath my dead weight
As I reached for the box
On the top shelf

Beretta

Clandestine meetings and microcassettes
Diner food never loses its charm
Lost since the irrevocable loss
But I found something to do with my hands

Combing for fibres and stray strands of hair
The mantel was wiped clean
No trace of trace evidence
But the heart says what the head won't

There's something brewing
In these small town sewers and wind-swept fields
Something dark, black as night
And it's not the coffee

Jazz singer, low-lit bar
Another drink down the hatch
Her voice sounds like small birds in springtime
And her mouth was once mauled
By an unforgiving blade

Boarding house steamer trunk
What secrets do you keep behind that antique lock?
A hammer will loosen your tongue
And the hardware store
Is only half a block from here

Teenage Knives

Death-threats to the heart
I climbed out the wishing well
Only to fall into the pit of despair

An affair
Just to keep the prosaic from desiccating
The price of the head given
In secondhand first cars
As the Zodiac strolls to the passenger-side window
The muzzle-flash nuzzle killing collecting of slaves
Will continue for now

Promises made as contingency plans
Until then I will decorate the war room
With lost photographs of regret and inaction

Ethereally Lost

Existence is relative
As the roadside flashes by
16mm smile
Cigarette smoke stutter
A stray strand of sun-bleach blonde hair
Upon a June-kissed cheek

Summer rain falls
Upon the dust-thick windshield
Another no-name town
Candy bars and gasoline
An icy stare from a taciturn local
And it's time to continue north
The Douglas firs sway
To the chords on the cassette tape
As the day starts to wash out
Let us never be found

Little Pools of Blood

A window sits open to the night
Beckoning to a creature
Blood-thirsty, and cloaked in shadow

A Ferris wheel stands dead still
Vines crawling its rusted framework
Once a home to kissing couples
It now plays perch
To cold-eyed crows

The burnt-out shell of a house sags
Still reeking of death
And the lost dreams of laughing families
A new home for wounded ghosts
Who will perpetually hurt and haunt
For time eternal

Coastal Fires

The Ferris wheel stood
Against a backdrop
Of black smoke firmament
A Halloween orange glow
Pervaded the whole coast
As Pacific Park burned

Cars crashed along the 101
Burst into flame on the 405
The U.S. Bank Tower
A beacon of darker times
A city of armless angels
Melting like overheated celluloid

Men slow danced with half-dressed starlets
Among the smouldering ruins
Raped them betwixt the sinking stones of Memorial Park
Pills were washed down with champagne
Or a bullet wound
To the upper soft palate

The inferno swept through
And left nothing in its wake
The ocean sighed with relief

In the End, All We Have is Nothing

American flags on fire
A bullet hole in the President's head
The White House is on fire
Funnels of black smoke rise from Capitol Hill
Bodies line the streets in their Sunday's best
God had other business to attend to

Landmines litter Central Park
Lost limbs scattered here and there
Gold watches glimmer in the perpetually burning sun
It doesn't get dark at all anymore
And the sewers are seeping onto the cracked sidewalks
Waging war against busted fire hydrants

We get what we deserve
And this is the final curtain call
As Lady Liberty topples into the harbour

Mercurial

Possessive pronouns
Check apostrophe placement
Undergarments discarded like loose teeth
Going in and out of fashion
Cuffed to the notched bedposts
Clutching cell bars in a death grip
I should have burnt your letter of resignation
Resigned to this shattered fate
Fucked by the whole football team
And it still wasn't enough

The Resurrection of an Undead Poet

On the eve of the eve of All Hallows' Eve
Thunder sang to me like church bells
Resonated in my unrepentant heart
Like an echo down a forgotten well

The lightning-bolt electrotherapy
Bestowed upon me a sense of clarity
The calm not before, but after the storm
Knowing I was exactly where I should be

Like that fateful night one April
Alone, but for manuscript and ink
It needs no further explanation
Than the words tattooed upon my hands

And So the Son of Satan Fell for the Preacher's Daughter

A gloom-filled day
A young lady, very beautiful, very intelligent
Helps her father build a small church
Somewhere in the middle of America
But darkness resides in her too-pure heart
And I am drawn
Like a moth to flame

But I am but a lowly man
Maladjusted, and crawling on all fours
Full moon reflected in both cunning eyes
And a thirst near insatiable

For now, we will live in these late-night missives
Candle-lit dreams, and shadow-filled desires

With these idle hands
And your work with children
My creeping fingers against those lovely legs
Let us lay between towering stones
In long, dead grass
With the dappled stained-glass light
Dancing across our perfect bones
Missing bodies tangled in fallen leaves
My lips upon that pallid neck
Lost in an ocean
Of strawberry-blonde hair

A Paler Moon

The bloodless years
Seem to stretch eternal
Sapped of vitality
Locked inside a dust-choked tomb
Tongue cracked and skin desiccated
The only sense, the dull throb of constant thirst
Long past memories of the moon
Are starting to now fade
It is possible for eternity to grow longer
For one such as I

Intuition

The scenes are scripted in my innards
Preordained passages that stab at my conscience like stilettos
There's no use in fighting

I carved her name into my wrist, but knew the scar wouldn't stay
These lovers only make for footnotes
Near forgotten by the end of the chapter
They hold little worth

Perhaps I'll die alone
With nothing but a small handful of achievements
But the play will play out how it will

Călărași

A tell-tale matchbook dropped
And quickly snatched back up
The letters ended up torn
A mess of shredded paper
In the bottom of a messenger bag

A mental photograph
Of red satin underwear
Clinging to a petite olive-skinned behind
She tasted like transgression
But felt like home

Familiars

These nocturnal creatures
Bestow wisdom and offer comfort
Lick my wounds
And watch over me while I sleep

For there are malicious men
That wish to drain the blood from these veins
Or burn this misshapen body upon the stake

Hear the screech of the barn owl
For me, he'll tear the eyes from your skull
Watch the haunting eyes of the wolf
He's watching you, and your throat
And all the world's black cats
Will scrap over your remains
So take heed
And stay away

Art Collector

Hotel room in fair Paris
She lays still upon the still-made bed
With legs only the French seem to possess

A penknife removed
From the right-hand bathrobe pocket
Takes the left ear off with ease

She is a masterpiece
Painted in brushstrokes of new blood
On a canvas of warm skin

Tie is straightened
Lint brushed from suit pants
And it's time to check-out
The museum opens at nine

Spectral Tides

Levitating above the city streets
Already haunted by the ghosts of the night before
Sparking cathedral fires
Sowing new cadavers in killing fields
Eyes do burn like funeral pyres
Mouth does twist in a carved-pumpkin smirk
Despair is such a pretty word
Never shall you forget the name I was given
And never shall you forget
Never shall you forget
What comes with the fall

Blacking Out the Eyes

The whole city grew dark
Snow swirled down the narrow streets
Lovers shivered in loose embraces
Elderly men poured another stiff drink
Most, if not all telephones were disconnected
And all lights – both interior and exterior
Flickered and died

The body of a small boy floated facedown
Down the colder canal
He'd been missing for the past week

The Hounds Have Caught the Scent

Pursuing you across continents
Obsessively anticipating
The taste of untouched flesh
No matter how well you hide yourself
In books of common prayer
I will find you
And take what is mine

Fenestra

This perpetual search
Has yielded no answers
Patient prayers for an escape route
Were lost in transmission
Or received and swiftly discarded

I haven't set foot outside
These cursed walls in years
Haven't even seen the sun
Meanwhile, time still ravages
With its inherent ferocity

I am consumed with obsession
Yet not knowing what I'd do
If I did indeed escape

What's Kept Alive

A vast woodland
Perpetually darkened
Suffused with amorphous mist
The air is thick and cool
Moisture palpable
This forest exists outside of time and place
Amongst the damp soil
And rustle of ferns
There lies lost
Decade-shed garments
A torn floral-patterned dress
Blue lace underwear
A lock of her hair
I kept in an empty chocolate box for years
Her scent hangs
A faint trace of skin and sweat
Sprawled across a narrow bed
In that childhood room
Crying out in excruciation
As the blood did come

The Casting Couch

Take a bow, and vow to never say goodnight
Behind the curtain, I'll be waiting
To grab and push you into the dressing room to
undress that gorgeous actress
Kiss the places the flashbulbs wished they illuminated
And be strangled to near-death by the B-roll
Slightly bleeding on the cutting room floor
Silhouetted she stands, knife in hand
Ready to carve this heart into the shape of love

Severed Heartstrings

Pulling coffin nails from hammered palms
Before climbing down from the burning cross
Cornfields sway in time to the death march snare drum
rattle
Windows of farm houses blink on and off in Morse code
verse
Has the ground opened up yet?
For I am afraid
That I've finally lost this fragile mind

Corpse Flower

Writing melancholy missives by candlelight
Wick & wax are waning
I should have died centuries ago
Buried in a coffin built from the staves of a wine barrel
Blooming late, like the Titan Arum
It comes as little surprise

Reading the Signs in Fallen Branches

An uncharacteristically stormy summer night
Crawled in without warning
Rattling the window frames
And wrenching leaves from wind-whipped trees
There is some not-insignificant meaning
Behind this surprise visit
Though, not much more is known
Aside from the unknown
And the intrinsic knowledge
That existence has to mean something more
Somewhere, sometime

A Burial

The shovels dig into fresh dirt
As she lies upon the dying grass
The wedding dress
A burial gown now

Soil is sprinkled
Upon her pretty face
Caught by eyelashes
Resting in the crevasse
Of her softened lips

I will mourn this solemn moment
But it was for the best

The Witch and the Well

Behind a dilapidated cottage
Ensconced in ivy and choking briar
Sits an older well
A darkened chasm leading straight down
Its depths unknown to any living mortal
It is said, that an old witch once lived there
She threw her own child down that very maw
After her husband ran off with a milkmaid
It is also said, that on uncertain nights
She still lurks in the shadows
Waiting patiently to push
An unsuspecting innocent
To their dampened death

A Soul to Keep, like a Secret Taken to the Grave

I watch from waxen shadows
A cloak of darkness shrouding this maladjusted man
Many years spent in the hitherto futile search
For one whose blood will flow with mine

A young lady stands
At the top of a stone staircase
Her eyes unlike any ever encountered
Her radiance enough to seep through the seams of this
patchwork heart
I am at the utter mercy of a creature so beautiful
That God himself weeps tears of joy at his true
masterpiece

Over mountain and across endless ocean
The soil in the casket shivers
Dracula has divorced his brides
And settled for one unfathomable true love

I shall kneel before you
And utter a solemn oath
To open the rusted cage inside of me
And unleash the beloved bats
To soar through the evening air
And send word
Of my future arrival

Six Foot Drifts

All has been buried
During the perpetual winter months
A splash of colour, only a harbinger of bad luck
Like blood on freshly fallen snow

Isolation brings one truly home
The stark morning light warming little
If anything at all
The fire burns deep into the coming night
And my heart shivers at the thought of you

Opinel

Sharp-edged dreams
Brown-haired girls and French lace
I cut the heart from the spread ribcage
Still beating, I held it in my hands
Before sinking incisors in

Blood-stained days
Locked in the unfaltering darkness
Of the village church crypt
I am home
Amongst these dry, brittle bones
Resting my troubled head
Upon the cold stone
Of the tomb's heavy lid

Standing on the Threshold of Madness

These rivers run with blood
To create in all its resplendent glory
Is to destruct utterly
The complete chaos of this dissolute mind
Is all that I have grown to know
Day in/Day out
I wither and thrive
Sharpen the blade on grinded teeth
And focus these blurry eyes
My poor body has had quite enough
And it anticipates the faint shuddering sigh
Of its parting spirit

Lost Writings

Discovered one fateful summer night
Bound with twine
And nestled inside an old hat box
At the back of the clothes closet
In a small cabin
On a lonely lakeside

Now that winter has set in proper
I know the truth behind those stolen words
A forewarning discarded
Then realization that came
Much too late

For it was I
That scrawled those hidden passages
Many years before

A Guillotine Moon

This dying season
Arrived in a flurry of missing child flyers
A fallen tricycle lay lopsided on the sidewalk
A lone wheel still spinning
"NOWHERE TO BE FOUND"
Should be painted on the welcome sign
Slowly rotting on the edge of town

With night comes
The click of locks turning over
Children ushered to well-lit rooms
Handguns well-oiled in bedside drawers
Heads robbed of sleep
Still, more do disappear

They lynched the elementary school caretaker
Skull struck-in with his own shovel
And shoved in the furnace
Handing candy out to kids
Used to be a respectable pastime

Somewhere, undiscovered bodies
Are piling high
Little eyes lost of light
This only happens every twenty years or so
And on the night of the town centennial
All shall be revealed

Nocturnal Skin

Standing lost amidst seasons
The snow falls upon the banks of the frozen Acheron
The twists of the twine of fate
Shall lead me to your door

Letters received from future days
Collect my scent to bottle in your basement
Drawing bridges and limbs aflame
While I draw blood
It is an acquired taste

Sleep has all but abandoned me
Watching over the grounds of this unhallowed place
The low throated growl of jet-black hound
And the hollow cries of wayward birds
Ring in the dying day

I will wander the endless hallways of your skull
Until I hold your elusive heart in my hands

Blessed in Blood that Flows Backward

Thank-you notes
Scrawled upon stray scraps of paper
The faint flickering spark
In eyes that understand nights like these
It's only fun if she writes back
And this one did

The late-night light
Burning in a second floor bedroom
Signals sent, and small animals delivered
Heart-shaped bone wrapped in Virginia creeper
I swallowed it whole
I couldn't stop smiling the whole time

House of Cats

Behind a tall brick wall
Overgrown with Virginia creeper
Sits a dilapidated house
Its tree-filled yard is not surprisingly overgrown
And if you happen to stop and peer
Through the ever-rusting wrought-iron front gate
Your inquisitive eyes will fall upon a score or more cats
Preening, stalking, playing, sleeping – they will pay you
no mind
They will be perched atop the weathered porch railing
Or curled in the morning sun
Upon the moss-dotted stone of the walk
Or padding along with the signature languor of their
species
Winged creatures beware!
Even mockingbirds don't dare brave these grounds
It is well-known local lore
That once an old spinster lived here
But she died
And was eaten by her cats

Gardens of Depravity

Falling to bloodied knees
Amongst the towering stone angels
And other assorted monolithic types

Feeding you the reddest apple in the bone orchard
As the fabled serpent hisses sibilant encouragement

The moon will spill its rotund secrets
To tell the truth
Is to disembowel

God turns his face away in mock shame
Though, this is nothing new

I whisper stories of nocturnal creatures
As you lay sated and spent

Winterbourne

Streams that flow with ice and cast leaves
Through the backyards of abandoned houses
Beneath dead grass soil
Lay bones of once-beloved dogs
Lost door keys, oxide-green pennies
And marriages long broken

These crooked waterways
All lead to the woods at the edge of town
Where they promptly disappear
Into dense shrubbery
And far darker secrets
Lurk beneath the ageless boughs

The Patron Saint of Suffering

She stands, scripture in hand
Crucifix in the other
Her eyes nothing but seared sockets
Taken by a lava-hot poker
Still, she never wavered
Never betrayed her still-beating heart
This is something many will never understand

Near-Death Experiences

I woke in a strange state
Dissected, and half-dressed
These useless limbs
Covered in cat-scratches
My tongue, so swollen from perpetual biting
That it filled my whole mouth

I walked amongst the tombs
Brushing grave-dirt from my pant legs
After the accident, I saw the light
But it was only the fire
Burning so fervent inside of me

And dear friend, you were there
Waiting at the ivy-entwined wrought-iron
To shake my hand and welcome my return
To the land of the living

Swallowing Keys

A bird in a cage
Upon the mist-thick sidewalk
A delicate yellow ribbon
Tied around its twig-thin leg
Somewhere nearby
A gramophone plays
Reading your long-sent letter
Over and over again
So much so
That its creases have worn completely through
And the ink is smudged and blurred
From forever falling tears
I don't know how to make sense anymore

Early Morning Mist-Shrouded Copse

Amongst faintly swaying fields
And frost-kissed trees
I meander meaninglessly
These bucolic senses
Are open to all that stirs
Under leaves, behind bluebells
In the early-dawn sky

The blackbird warns half the forest
And the fox already long knows
In the gentle gilded beams of sunlight
Something is caught sight of
Lily white skin, and red-hued hair
Two small horns
Sprouting from a pretty head
The swiftly-vanishing bare body
Of a small young girl
Entwined with strands of ivy

This will never be spoken of
But instead cherished
Until the last breath
Rattled upon the deathbed
Of a dying peasant

Six by Eight

I got lost for years
Inside the catacombs
Of my own cranium
Pacing endlessly
Muttering incoherent incantations
Trying in vain to invoke
Some kind of omniscience

A painting hung
In the orange-brown of long dried blood
Aging like Dorian
Burning like Joan of Arc
What little left I had
I poured into creation
A piece of me curling up and dying
With every last line

Her Card Is Death

Eternally endearing
So much so
That I struggle to unearth the words
Perhaps I shall leave it up to the Ouija board
To spell it all out for me
The whiskey glass, or the otherworldly advice
Of the long departed
It is all just seeking solace in spirits

I would gaze into this antique mirror
'til the sun comes up
If it meant I could stare into those azure eyes
And get so lost
I could never find my way back home

River Stones

A deserted bank
Lined with hunched willows in winter
A pale hand
Reaches into the still water
Stirs dead leaves
Searching for something
Others have long forgotten

The levels will rise
With the next rain
Wash away what was never found
Along with her bare body

Come spring
The wild cherry blossoms
Will fall
Upon a new stone

Memorial Plaques

Hidden meanings
Scrawled in the backs of library books
Pushed to the back of the shelf
And found some sleepy Sunday

Maybe I can slip the knife in
To further investigate this enigma
A girl's name below a stanza from Dante
The reference section should yield answers
Or at least kill some time

An address written on a scrap of paper
A movement in an upstairs window
A light blinks out, then on, then out again
A silhouette disappears

Reappears a moment later in the front doorway
Beckons with a curled finger
Our Virgil is found

Ink & Ash

Setting down more wayward lines
As the trees dance in death
Outside the bedroom window
The moon has set in winter night
I continue to scrawl
Amongst the wisps of exhaled breath

The light burns long in shadowed smoke
Heart-beat slows to a feline crawl
I long for the warmth of blood
That old spill seems far removed
Like teeth lost in necks and thighs
The smell of regret used to ring in the day of rest
Now it all just smoulders

Catholic Candles

The cathedral lights radiate through the hanging branches
They catch on my coat as I push between
A moss-covered statue of a weeping angel stands to my
right
And a crumbling mausoleum to my left
Leaves crunch underfoot

Push slowly open the doors
At the end of the aisle
She kneels at the altar
A lit candle cradled in her fragile hands
Mine begin to shake

Through the Small Hours, a Delicate Heart Does Beat

A full moon hangs high
She leaves her window unlocked at night
Complete with a small hand-written invitation of sorts

The faint stir of the curtains
A soft chill upon the cheek
After dawn breaks
You will never have to be alone
For as far as eternity does stretch

Summer Legs

The susurration of corn fields
Omnipresent and lulling
Skin is blood-warm beneath the floral-patterned fabric
of her sundress
The roof tiles are sagging
Windows thick with timeless dust
The sunlight pools on the creaking floorboards
Strawberry-blonde hair billows in a silken cloud
So exquisitely lost
Longing to never find our way back home

Watershed

Forever searching for that definitive moment
Where time will shatter and be born again
Replenishing the shallow bloodstream
That crawls through sunken veins

Bones, once fractured
Will reform strong as this will
Heads, once severed
Sewn back to the neck
Darkness dissipates
Now nothing but a faint shadow
Imprinted on the back of this mind

The morning sun will spill
Through the slightly open window
And creep across bare skin
Like gilded fingers of a once forgotten God

Stop Dying

An attic room
Whitewashed doll's houses
& blood-warm lace
A low painted ceiling
On which to hang my sins
Like cut-out cardboard stars

Nail shut the door
It's either you, or her
Wry smile & knowing eyes
Set in skin like virgin silk
Yours are sunken like shipwrecks
And where the ink hasn't set
You're yellowed like old parchment

Close the casket
& live
Piece by fragile piece

And We Always Seem to Return to That Same Old Month

The October sky explodes
Shards of stars burning across space
Standing here,
Holding the hand of a strange girl
Can't help but feeling like this has happened
Somewhere/sometime before

Rebirth

It begins when the door shuts
And the light from the desk-lamp spills out
Onto books and rumpled bed sheets
Sometime in the middle of the night

About Benjamin Blake

Benjamin Blake was born in the July of 1985, and grew up in the small town of Eltham, New Zealand. He is the author of the poetry and prose collections *A Prayer for Late October*, *Southpaw Nights*, and *Reciting Shakespeare with the Dead*. His debut novel, *The Devil's Children*, was published in October of 2016.

Find more of his work at www.benjaminblake.com.

Also available:

RADIX OMNIUM MALUM by Mike Chinn
ISBN: 978-0-9957173-0-5

SHADES by Joseph Rubas
ISBN: 978-0-9935742-9-0

THE CHAMELEON MAN by David Williamson
ISBN: 978-0-9935742-9-3

A PLACE OF SKULLS by David Ludford
ISBN: 978-0-9935742-6-9

HAUNTED GRAVE by Ezeiyoke Chukwunonso
ISBN: 978-0-9935742-3-8

INTO THE DARK by Andrew Jennings
ISBN: 978-0-9935742-5-2

TOUGH GUYS by Adrian Cole
ISBN: 978-0-9935742-2-1

CLASSIC WEIRD 2 selected by David A. Riley
ISBN: 978-0-9932888-4-5

OTHER VISIONS OF HEAVEN AND HELL by Jessica Palmer
ISBN: 978-0-9935742-1-4

A SAUCERFUL OF SECRETS by Andrew Darlington
ISBN: 978-0-9935742-0-7

THE WINTER HUNT AND OTHER STORIES
by Steve Lockley & Paul Lewis
ISBN: 978-0-9932888-9-0

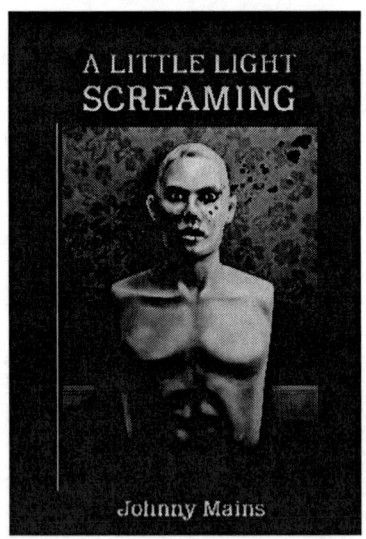

A LITTLE LIGHT SCREAMING by Johnny Mains
ISBN: 978-0-9932888-5-2

ENGLAND 'B': 90 MINUTES OF HELL by Richard Staines
ISBN: 978-0-9932888-7-6

AND NOBODY LIVED HAPPILY EVER AFTER by Kate Farrell
ISBN: 978-0-9932888-8-3

FISHHEAD: THE DARKER TALES OF IRVIN S. COBB

ISBN: 978-0-9935742-4-5

KITCHEN SINK GOTHIC: Selected by David and Linden Riley
ISBN: 978-0-9932888-3-8

WILL ANYONE FIGURE OUT THAT THIS IS A REPACKAGED FIRST COLLECTION? by Johnny Mains
ISBN: 978-0-9574535-7-9

BLACK CEREMONIES by Charles Black
ISBN: 978-0-9574535-5-5

HIS OWN MAD DEMONS:
DARK TALES FROM DAVID A. RILEY
ISBN: 978-0-9574535-8-6

THEIR CRAMPED DARK WORLD by David A. Riley
ISBN: 978-0-9574535-9-3

THE HEAVEN MAKER AND OTHER GRUESOME TALES
by Craig Herbertson
ISBN: 978-0-9932888-2-1

GOBLIN MIRE by David A. Riley
ISBN: 978-0-9574535-4-8

THINGS THAT GO BUMP IN THE NIGHT
selected by Douglas Draa and David A. Riley
ISBN: 978-0-9574535-6-2

CLASSIC WEIRD selected David A. Riley
ISBN: 978-0-9574535-3-1

MOLOCH'S CHILDREN by David A. Riley
ISBN: 978-0-9932888-1-4

Check our website:

http://paralleluniversepublications.blogspot.co.uk/

CPSIA information can be obtained
at www.ICGtesting.com
Printed in the USA
LVOW12s1530130917

548603LV00001B/202/P